From altitude comes perspective. And .... Bach is in need of per-
spective when he sets out to solve the design problems troubling his
Piper Cub. But when he takes wing on the simple course from question
to answer, from necessity to invention, his journey takes an unexpected
turn . . . into an uncharted territory where flying machines are dreams
taken aloft by men in leather helmets . . . where a mysterious woman pro-
vides the astonishing answers to his unspoken questions . . . and the year
is 1923. . . .

An enthralling flight into the realm of possibility, *Out of*
My Mind follows Richard Bach on an unforgettable journey
to the creative heyday of the Saunders-Vixen Aircraft
Company. And in this profoundly resonant tale, crafted in
the spirit of the classic *Jonathan Livingston Seagull*, we are
reminded of a powerful truth that makes the spirit soar:
that although our dreams may lie beyond the limits of
time, space, and belief, they are never beyond reach. . . .

OUT OF MY MIND

Delta
Trade Paperbacks

Out
of My
Mind

The Discovery of Saunders-Vixen

RICHARD BACH

Illustrations by K. O. Eckland

A Delta Book
Published by
Dell Publishing
a division of
Random House, Inc.
1540 Broadway
New York, New York 10036

Cover illustration by K.O. Eckland.

Delta® is a registered trademark of Random House, Inc., and the
colophon is a trademark of Random House, Inc.

ISBN: 0-385-33490-7

Reprinted by arrangement with William Morrow and Company, Inc.

Manufactured in the United States of America

Published simultaneously in Canada

September 2000

10 9 8 7 6 5 4 3 2

To Tink

Out
of My
Mind

I

The problem was the door. It wouldn't stay open.

On a Piper Cub, the door is in two pieces—one wide trapezoid for the top half, with plexiglass for a window, another for the bottom half, covered in yellow fabric, the same as the rest of the airplane. The bottom half works fine because as soon as it's unlatched it drops right down, and the weight of it keeps it there.

The top half, though, pivots upward, and there's a weak little catch to hold the door open when pilot or passenger enters or leaves the cockpit. The catch will hold the door open while taxiing and through takeoff.

The view from a Cub with the door open is widescreen technicolor three-dimension stereo sound, the grass and treetops dropping away, one's heart soaring above. Wind pours by, a '28 convertible ratcheting down its mountain curve with a side missing, instead of the top. To splash in that wind . . . That's why people like me enjoy messing around with airplanes.

Except the top half of the door slammed shut. When I flew any faster than 65 miles per hour, the pressure of the wind overpowered the latch, and *stam!* there I was in a half-closed cabin, cut off from my river of wind. Vexing, vexing.

I thought about it for days, after I met the problem. It haunted me.

At work, trying to write, there it was, turning slowly in space between my eyes and the computer screen, the image of that latch. A bigger latch of the same type wouldn't answer. The force of the wind increases as the square of the speed, I knew. The door would slam down at 70 mph instead of 65.

Remove the door? No, I thought. Sometimes, in the winter, in rainstorms . . . I don't want the side of the airplane open forever.

A hook, a screen-door hook. On an airplane? What would I screw it into, the wing fabric?

Drifting down the aisles of the hardware store, the image drifting with me. Not magnets, not pressure catches, not window locks. Nothing would work. There was no way to anchor the latch to the wing. The image faded when I went to sleep.

Next morning early, not even awake, there floated the picture of that latch again. I groaned

5

at the sight. Was it going to follow me through yet another day, taunting me with my mechanical incompetence?

When I looked again, though, looked carefully, the latch was not the same as it had been the day before. Not the same at all. It was fastened to the wing by two modified expansion screws, drilled not into the fabric, but into the aluminum wing rib behind the fabric. Plenty of bearing surface there, supporting a different latch design, one that slips over the doorframe itself, on and off at a touch, yet holds the door like a vise.

That picture floated in early light just long enough for me to understand, then it was gone. No image in the air, no problem humiliating me, no nothing. Empty air.

I didn't need to be prodded. I grabbed the pad at my bedside, slashed down a drawing of the new design. Work? Of course it will work! Why didn't the Piper Cub factory design a latch like this in 1939?

In a matter of hours, the fitting was complete, the brass of the latch neatly drilled, the little expansion screws cut to just two tabs each, screwed tightly into place on the wing.

I pulled the airplane from the hangar, launched it into the air, dived to 110 mph. The door unflinching, solid as the wing itself.

I'm not incompetent, I'm a design genius. Can't wait! to park alongside the next Cub I see, to examine its flimsy door latch, whisper, "Too bad . . ." to a pilot who would know full well what was too bad, who would give anything, trade her finest flying gloves for a door latch that halfway worked.

And that was the end of the story. In time happiness with my door latch melted into general overall happiness, and today if I had to draw the latch from memory I probably couldn't do it.

Not a month later, though, it happened again.

It seems that I had not quite tightened the

7

oil cap on the engine of the Cub, and one day flying high over the forest, I struck a sudden downdraft, a sharp jolt to the airplane. At the same instant I noticed a canary fly past the open door.

"That's strange," I said aloud, looking back at the yellow speck dwindling from sight. "Why would a canary be flying this high, and over such a desolate place?" I finally concluded that it must have been an escaped canary, free at last, flexing its little wings in delight.

After a few minutes I noticed some drops of oil on the lift strut just beside the open door. Then many more drops. Then oil on the right side of the windshield, then oil in sheets down the side of the airplane.

I wondered, turning toward a wide level hayfield. Have we broken an oil line? What's going on?

Then it dawned. That was no canary, over the forest, that was my oil cap! That was my oil filler cap, painted canary yellow, and this was my engine oil being sucked from the topless tank! It was time to land.

That evening. An oil cap turns in the air, between me and my computer screen. How do you make sure, Richard, that you never lose an oil cap again? Some flight in the future you will not quite tighten that dipstick down steel-solid, you will see a canary again and whisper, Oh, no . . .

I can't bolt it down, or screw it down with a fastener that knowing me will likely end up in the oil tank. There has to be some way of securing . . . But it's designed simply to be screwed tight. And I know that someday I will forget to tighten it. How to keep the cap from turning loose, taking off for one last flight on its own, solo?

I woke early, before morning light, and found the foggy image as it had been the night before, floating in front of me, problem unsolved. Yet I watched carefully, thinking nothing. Just watched. Patiently.

And then a strange thing happened. There

9

was a rustle in the air, the image dissolved and a different oil cap appeared. And as I watched, for the splittest of seconds, I saw a form behind the hardware, a lovely human face, glimpsed as one might glimpse through glass at the moment the mail is delivered. The face of the carrier of the mail.

In that instant there was a flash of startlement as her eyes met mine, watching; her breath caught, and she was gone.

Left turning, glistening in air, was an oil cap with a thong attached, leather like a bootlace. One end of the thong was attached to the cap by a tiny wire connector, the other end was lashed to the cowl clip just below the right rear engine cylinder. Clip in place, I saw, there was no way for that assembly to go sailing off. It could perhaps be jerked loose by some tornado, but it wouldn't leave the Cub unless the front half of the airplane ripped away with it.

Simple, conclusive, obvious fix.

I was in the workshop by evening, drilling a

tiny hole for the connector in the side of the
cap, inserting a wire to hold the thong, lashing
the thong to the cowl clip, fitting it into place
on the Cub. It worked perfectly. Even when I
loosened the cap, yanked hard to pull it from
the oil tank, it wouldn't slide more than an
inch from the opening, the dipstick still in the
filler tube, the thong unyielding. Yes! Never
another canary!

Walking back to the house that evening, I
fell to wondering. Why a leather thong? I
thought. Why not steel cable? Everybody in avi-
ation uses steel cable, nowadays, why had the
idea come with leather?

As I puzzled that out, thinking back to the

moment the solution had appeared, I saw again the lovely fraction-of-a-second face, a wooden draftsman's pencil tucked casually in that dark hair, the surprise deep in brown eyes as they met mine. And the instant vanishment, thereafter.

Somebody said the words, in my voice, as I stopped on the path, remembering. "Who? Was? *That?*"

I closed my mouth, but the question didn't stop. How could I have forgotten those eyes? That wasn't just morning insight, solving my airplane problems, there had been a woman there!

You don't need to be a quantum mechanic to imagine the problem I wrestled that evening, and the next day, and the one after that. Just because something happens in a split second doesn't mean it hasn't happened, as any clay pigeon will tell you.

And I had been scattered in as many pieces by that single shot. There was no mistake. Our recognition for random objects fails, I'm told, at exposures of less than half a second. Of geometrical objects, at less than a fiftieth of a second. But our perception of a smile will remain from a flash as short as a thousandth of a second, so sensitive are our minds to images of the human face.

I flew the Cub next afternoon, and from the ground it must have been a lazy sight, the little airplane turning slowly, lemon-color wings relaxed on the wind, barely a whisper from the engine.

It was not lazy for me. I could fly this airplane anywhere in the world, I thought. With special big fuel tanks, there is no place on the planet that a Piper Cub cannot go. But where to fly to find the person who handed me that simple design?

I throttled the engine back a few hundred revolutions, to zero thrust, the propeller turning just fast enough to pull its own weight. At this power the Cub became a sun-painted

13

glider, a thirty-foot sailing kayak adrift in the sky. It rose and fell gently on the waves of air that passed beneath its wings.

If my lovely messenger existed somewhere, why didn't I see her solve the first problem, why didn't I see her float the door latch to me, special-delivery? I frowned, remembering.

When I saw the latch, there had been no hint of a messenger. Just the message itself, an elegant solution to a problem held in mind. It had been waiting for me to open my eyes from sleep and notice.

The Cub turned, soft and slow as a seabird, over farmland set checker-quilt gold in the afternoon. Following the purr of its little engine, it lifted fifty feet on a swell of warm air, sailed through, invisible wake stirring the sky behind, plowed gently down through the cooler trough that followed.

It was a lovely day for sailing aloft. My spirit was elsewhere.

Of course. I didn't see her the first time be-

cause she had already come and gone, the messenger had left her package and moved on. The
second time, though, the customer was expecting mail, I had been waiting for it. When we
wait long enough by our mailbox, I thought,
should we be surprised when the carrier ap-
pears?

It made perfect sense, the problem was
solved. That's who she was, that's why I saw her.

Answers, of course, solve nothing. The
mystery was no longer how to discover designs
to fix my airplane. The mystery had turned as
deep as the sky itself: where did those designs
come from?

A long time ago I learned that everything is
exactly as it is for a reason. The crumb is on our
table not only as a reminder of this morning's
cookie, it is there because we have chosen not to
remove it. No exceptions. Everything has a reason, and the tiniest detail is a clue.

From altitude, literally, comes perspective.
The cockpit of a little airplane, once it becomes

home, is a perfect high nest in which to solve problems.

The surprise in her eyes. If she's a carrier, why would she be startled to come upon the ad-dressee, waiting?

The Cub drifted around a tiny cloud. Later this afternoon the little puff would be a giant: massive, towering. For now it was a play-ful fluffy sheep, rushing at my wings.

She'd be startled if it never happens, I thought. She expects her customers to sleep while the mail's put up. When one in a thou-sand is bolt awake, staring at her when she ar-rives, of course she's startled.

The pencil in her hair. If I were her, why would I keep a pencil there?

Because I use a pencil nearly every minute of the day. Because I use a pencil so often that it's wasting time to reach down and pick it up from a desktop.

But . . . why do I use a pencil so much?

Off in the distance, half a mile away, a

Cessna training plane. I rocked the Cub's wings: Hello, I have you in sight. To my surprise the Cessna's wings rocked back. It's an old aviator's custom, not often followed, these days.

Why do I need a pencil so often that I would tuck it in my hair? Because I make many lines on paper. Because I'm drawing, all the time.

Because I'm a designer. Of parts. For airplanes!

Can't be, I thought. Designers don't use pencils. They use computers. They sketch with computer-assisted design machines, with a mouse and a screen. If you don't use CAD, you're no designer, you have been trampled by progress.

By now, the ground warming, the swells in the ocean of air grew larger. Once in a while a wave of rising heat broke under the nose of the Cub with a shudder and jolt, showering sprays of sky-drops ten feet in the air.

Her hair, I thought, gathered in dark full-

17

ness and pinned at the back of her neck, she's not doing that to look old-fashioned. She is all business, this person, she is not pretending to be what she is not. There's a reason . . .

I relived that moment. What other clues? What had I missed? Her mouth open a little, in surprise. A white collar, buttoned primly, a dark oval brooch set in silver at her throat. The wooden pencil, unpainted, no eraser, ready to use. Yellow light in the background, the color of sunlight on wood. Nothing more. The lovely eyes.

That was no glare-white cubicle of some conglomerate's CAD division, I had seen. It was almost as if . . . Why would an all-business, efficient designer use a pencil so often that she would keep it . . .

She would use a pencil, I mused, because she had no computer.

Why did she have no computer? Reason for everything. Why the prim collar, the brooch, why would she want to dress so differently from others? Why the yellow light?

In the lazy Cub, half a mile in the air, I sat bolt upright.

My designer doesn't have CAD because CAD hasn't been invented. She wears old-fashioned clothes not to be different from the people around her, but to be the *same!* She looks like dear yesterday *because she's from a different time!*

All at once my little sail was over. I cut the power to the engine, rolled the Cub inverted and fell like a cliff-diver, toward the earth. I had to get back on the ground, shake off the misty otherworld of flight. I had to find if what I knew could possibly be the truth.

2

Whoever said " 'Tis the journey be the plea-sure, and nae t'arrive" was not en route to the other side of time.

A week after my flight in the Cub, I had moved not an inch closer to the place from which my airplane-part images had come. Not once again did I see the face of that lovely messenger.

That I was curious, that I wanted to peer

into her world was my problem, she seemed to be telling me; she was not the least willing to help me in a scheme unauthorized by her employer. For all the evidence I could gather in a week's crafty planning to draw her out, she didn't exist.

I curled evenings on the couch in front of my little fireplace, staring into the flames. When I half-closed my eyes, the light seemed as well to be flickering in some other place, a room with high-back leather chairs around. I couldn't see the chairs but sensed them, sensed others in the room, an indistinct murmur of voices, sensed someone walking by, not noticing, not far away. I saw only the fire, and shadows in a room that was not mine.

I shook my head, and the vision, fragile, shattered.

After a while an answer occurred to me. To lure her back, all I need do is to present her with a problem to be solved! And when she approaches with its solution, I'll be there to tell her wait.

At once I set to designing a new set of wheel chocks for the airplane. Did I need something that folded from a collapsed travel-state to a geometry that would hold the Cub against a windstorm? I imagined some pitiful chocks, floated them in my mind before lights-out. Bait.

Nothing. Come morningtide, the same flimsy ratty things were still there. I trashed them. Next evening, I asked her help inventing a little something to keep the rain out of the fuel tank, something besides an inverted tomato-paste can. Perhaps something of machined aluminum?

Silence. No response. To pretend-problems, to designs for wheel chocks where blocks of wood do best, to gas cap covers for an airplane that's always hangared, to unfinished assemblies whose true purpose was to lure her back into sight, she remained aloof. Each floated in front of me in the morning as it had the evening before, lures only, about which I didn't care save they might show me her eyes once more.

Two weeks hinted that craftiness would go years without response, and I fretted about that, apologized in the quiet dawn for my wrong track. I had surrounded my wish to see her again in a mantle of guile. What did I expect from deceit, that she'd show up, trusting, say hello from one side of time to the other?

A month after the event, still I stared evenings into the fire, old clock on the mantel, rebuilding tok by tok what had happened. Those designs had come from somewhere, each of them were installed this moment on my happily three-dimensional Piper J-3C, hangared in the winter of 1998.

I did not make them up, I did not have a clue how to solve the problems when I had left them for sleep. They were not holographic

pranks by a neighbor aiming through the dawn with a secret laser projector. They were not hallucinations. Simple, they were, but ingenious . . . they were working designs that solved real problems.

Further, I thought, they carried none of the trappings of now. No exotic materials or processes, no subtle liability warnings, nothing that hinted a computer database for puzzled mechanics.

Her face haunted me. Matter-of-fact, businesslike, focused so completely on the work, on doing her job so well that one glance at me watching blanked her, threw her off-line.

I studied the flames, the shadows dancing. There is a place. There is a room, as solid and warm and unchanging in its world as this room is in mine. It is not Here, it is When . . .

"Very well, Gaines, have a go in the morning, if you'd like. Take Eff-Zed-Zed. Mind you bring her back in one piece."

It wasn't spoken aloud, it wasn't someone talking by the couch, it was the everyday naturalness of the words in my head that startled, the glass edge of that simple sentence sliced into my quiet. I felt it tingle at the back of my neck.

"What?" As if by surprising it, shouting in my tomb-silent parlor I'd earn some answer. *"What?"*

The clock paced on, carefully measuring time.

Alone in the house, I didn't care who heard. *"Eff-Zed-Zed?"*

No answer.

"*Gaines?*"

Tok; tok; tok; tok;

"*Are you playing games with me?*" I was seized
with yearning rage.

"*What's the game?*"

3

After weeks, I knew the obvious. I was not going to solve my test by pushing, or beating on it, or begging it to do something that it would not do. The question occurred: Could the search for a working door latch have driven me out of my mind? A dead-end street, that fancy. How would I know?

Last-ditch, in the rare times when things are not going well for me, I drag my sleeping bag out to the Cub, start the engine, fly over a horizon toward sunset, land in a field of grass for the night. Then I watch the sky, listen for voices of friends I cannot see.

Sometimes the only way to win is to surrender. And in surrender I laid myself in the grass, under the wing of my little air-boat, and asked the stars.

"If I am meant to understand what is happening to me," I whispered toward Arcturus, "show me what I need to know. I don't understand what to do next. It's yours. I let it go."

The lightest of breeze whispered back, wind through grass that had sighed for a thousand years. "Let go."

4

I lay in the night, darkness a cool blanket tucked about me, breathing slowly, slowly, and deep. Relax. Let go. It is not your mystery. You do not have to solve anything. What is, is. Your job: Be quiet. Your mission: Be still.

Deep air in; wait; slow air out. Long slow wait. Cool air in; wait; warm air out. My only responsibility; is to be.

The dark air swirled about me, through me,

the night became me. A curious feeling of lift-
ing, going light and melting the same moment,
infinitely heavy, into the earth.

While I watched, barely noticing, the scene
began to slide, about me, the way a night view
slides outside when our train begins to move.
Barest whisper of acceleration, soundless in the
dark. Don't care, Richard, I thought, it makes
no difference. Allow. Accept. So soothing was
the thought that it didn't matter that the walls
of my space were changing. All was well.

I breathed calm, slow, uncaring, and before
me, a gentle glow. When the walls eased noise-
less to a stop, it was daylight.

I was resting on emerald grass, under a deep
sky. The Cub and the night were gone. I lay
near a path on a rise of ground, reminding myself slow, no hurry, take your time. So carefully
I lifted myself to sit and, later, to stand. In that
moment, distant rising thunder behind me. I
turned and looked.

The roof of the hangar was a long shallow arch, fifty feet above the ground. Beneath the arch, a wide band of windowpanes, hundreds of windowpanes. Beneath the windows, giant doors, thirty feet tall. The thunder, deep and low, was the sound of one of those massive doors, rolling open.

I watched, unmoving.

Voices across the distance, unintelligible. A laugh. The men wore white coveralls. They're mechanics, I thought, then rephrased: They're ground engineers. The deep rumble continued, a tall black rectangle of the interior widening. Presently the rumbling stopped and the door stood open.

A bird sang nearby, four sudden notes to the sun, a song I did not recognize.

Then from within the hangar appeared an aircraft, a small open biplane, gradually pulled into the day. Silver, the wings, the color of metal flaked from a lathe. A fuselage of dusty

39

mint, silver again the surfaces of the rudder and elevators. A fitter pulled at each wingtip, one at the tail pushed a dolly upon which rested the machine's tailskid.

Their voices carried on the breeze, though distance mixed the sound, and not a word could I understand.

Airports I know and I love, airports have always been home to me, no matter where on the planet I might be. Not thinking, then, I began to walk along the path, toward the hangar.

It's not quite a Thomas-Morse Scout, I thought. It's an Avro 504? A machine I have never seen in person, knew it only from pictures. Am I in England?

Softly rolling countryside, a mile-wide square of level turf around the hangar. No runways, no taxiways. Not an airport, would they call it. An aerodrome.

The path curved right, then left again. The hangar was screened for a while by hedge bor-

dering the pathway. I felt anxious, with the sight
of it veiled, as if should I lose that compass I'd
be tumbled in darkness.

But a few minutes later the hedge dropped
away to a row of careful flowers planted, prim-
ula. Primrose, they might say here.

By now the hangar was huge at my left.
Fronting it was a building of wood and stone, to
the left of that, a car-park. That is where I
stopped again. There were seven motor vehicles
on the gravel. I did not recognize a single one.
Small, most of them, squarish, metals dull and
metals gleaming. Automobiles have never been
my passion, I wish I could describe them better.
But even I could tell the era from which they
came . . . a time post-1910 and pre-1930. A
gawky motorcycle, as much a motorbike,
painted olive green, balanced on a frail kick-
stand.

The path skirted the car-park, became a
cobblestone sidewalk became a short flight of

wooden steps became a covered walkway to a large building set square against the hangar. A sign in carved wood by the steps to the walkway, the first words I had seen in this place:

SAUNDERS-VIXEN AIRCRAFT COMPANY, LTD.

5

Before the steps I paused, my hand on the railing. I knew that my body rested dreaming back in the grass, breathing deeply, under stars. I knew I could wake, any time I wished. I knew that everything in sight was my own imagination. But long since had I trashed the phrase "only imagination." Convinced that everything in the physical world is imagination dressed to look solid, I was not about to wake from this place, or discount it.

It is as real, and as unreal, as my waking world, I thought. All I need to know is where am I, and what does this place mean?

The door opened at the end of the wooden walkway, under the SAUNDERS-VIXEN sign, and a young man appeared, carrying a roll of onionskin paper. I knew that he could not see me, as I didn't belong in his time. I was seeing this place in my mind, not affecting it in any way.

I studied him as he walked toward me. He wore a tweedy suit, subtle beige crosshatch, white shirt-collar, dark tie at his neck, with a sort of gold-wire device to hold the points of the collar down. There was what looked like an engine-oil stain on the sleeve of the coat.

Fair-haired, cheerful, whistling for a moment under his breath, the face of an earnest student of business. I watched unmoving as he approached, taking in every detail. Two pencils and a fountain pen in his pocket. Too young to be an executive, I thought, was he a draftsman, an engineer of some kind? He slowed at the top of the steps, appeared almost to see me, as if he had a sense of my presence.

Something of an intellectual, I guessed, he doesn't spend much time outdoors. The air of an unkempt, a not quite ordered mind.

Instead of walking through me, he stopped, looked directly at me.

"Good morning," he said. "Excuse me, please?"

I started. "Me?"

"Yes. May I pass?"

"Certainly! Of course," I said. "By all means. Sorry . . ."

"Thank you."

The onionskin roll brushed against my sweater with a crackly scrape.

In a moment, as I recovered from my surprise, came the kick and bang of the motorbike engine starting behind me, and when I

47

turned, the young man was pulling on a set of goggles. No helmet, just the old-fashioned goggles. The engine idled, puffing irregular blue smoke.

He looked at me for a moment, expressionless, more listening to the engine than paying attention to me, then nodded and with a wave and a burst of throttle was on his way down the path to the road. Presently the noise died off into the shrubbery and it was quiet again.

Saunders-Vixen, I thought. No airplane company I've ever heard of, yet here it is.

I walked up the stairs, hearing the sound: shoes on wood. Not ghostly, not invisible.

Inside the door, an office anteroom, a low counter, a dark wooden desk, a receptionist standing at an oaken file cabinet, turning as I entered.

"Good morning, sir," she said. "Welcome to Saunders-Vixen."

She was dressed not unlike the woman from

my psychic post office. Long dark skirt, white blouse of many buttons, of many tight pleats, a small coral cameo at her neck. Dark blonde hair, pulled tightly to a bun at the back.

"Good morning." I smiled. "You're expecting me? You know who I am?"

"Let me guess," she said, pretending solemn. "You're an aeroplane designer? It has taken you a long time to find us? Now you have? You'd like to visit the plant?"

I had to laugh. "I'm not the first?"

She pressed a button. "Mr. Derek Hawthorne," she said, "you have a visitor at the main desk."

Then she looked up. "Not the first by any means, sir. It's hard to find us, it's not impossible."

There was a muffled airy burst of an engine starting at full throttle outside, then cut off, then full throttle again. A rotary engine, I knew. They had started the Avro. This would be . . . 1918?

A door behind the desk opened, a young man entered. Dark hair, the broad, open face of one with nothing to hide. He was dressed in tweeds, a white silk scarf, a leather flying jacket, and he saw me listening to the sound. "That's the Morton, starting up. Old engine. It's full go or it's off."

His handshake was firm. Years as an assembler, I thought. "Richard Bach," I said.

"Derek Hawthorne, of Saunders-Vixen, Limited, at your service. Have you visited before?" He glanced at the receptionist, who shook her head, a silent no.

"You're in 1923 parallel, of course." He knew I'd miss it, saw my question. "Not your past, but running alongside your time. Sounds complicated, but it isn't, really."

Derek Hawthorne lifted a leather coat from a peg near the door, handed it to me. "I'd imagine you'll be wanting this. It's a bit chilly, yet."

In imagination, I thought, anything can happen. This was the first time, however, that my imaginations had imagined me, as well.

I took the coat, a tag sewn in gold letters at the neckband, and I read: THIS JACKET WORN IN GRATEFUL MEMORY OF THE DEAR ANIMAL WHO GAVE HER EARTHLY LIFE TO PROTECT AN AVIATOR FROM WIND AND COLD.

I looked at him. He nodded, no smile.

No smile, silent thanks to a cow unmet, I slipped it on.

Hawthorne opened the door from the reception room on a long hallway leading to the hangar, a hallway paneled in dark wood, hung with paintings of aircraft. "You'll want to see our machines, I'll wager."

51

"I would. But a question?"

"Of course. We may seem a little mysterious, at first. We're not."

We walked past a number of doors, off the hallway: Sales, Marketing, Accounting, Engines & Systems, Airframe Design, CAD. It was at the instant we were passing the last that the door opened, and there, glancing up, pencil tucked in hair, eyes dark as night, the face that I had seen from another time.

"Oh!" she said.

That instant, the world disappeared.

6

As though I had tumbled from a roof, I jarred awake in the hayfield, under stars twinkling beyond the wing of the Cub. The night was cold as steel.

"Hai!" I said, a ball of frustration. "Na!"

I grabbed flashlight and journal, shoved the cold away, wrote everything I had seen and heard: the morning in England, the hangars of the Saunders-Vixen Aircraft Company, the car-park, the building, desk, counter, receptionist, Derek Hawthorne, every detail. The face that had blown the world away.

I shivered, reached outside my sleeping bag for the Cub's engine cover, wrapped it around me.

It was a delicious memory, that time, that face, and I raced to return to my imagining.

But though I gradually warmed, under the engine cover, all I found in my mind were questions. What is Saunders-Vixen? Why does it exist? What does it have to tell me? Who is this woman? *How do I go back?*

Questions, all the way through dawn. No answers.

7

He had said it so matter-of-factly that I pre-
tended it was a matter of fact. There is a dimension, drifting parallel to our own, in which it is
still a sort of 1923.

In this dimension exist hangars and offices,
motorcycles and auto-cars, people who earn
their living by working with airplanes: designing them, building them, putting them into
operation, selling and servicing them. There

doubtless exist farms and villages and cities as well, but all I had imagined for sure were the facilities of Saunders-Vixen Aircraft Company, Ltd., and the people who worked there.

There were curious differences. It was not our 1923. The women's fashion, for instance, was more our 1890 than our 1920. Yet their awareness and their quiet satisfaction that they live in a parallel world to ours was considerably more advanced than mine, at such an idea.

Writing stopped, Cub back in the hangar, rain pelting the roof, I stared once again at the fire from the comfort of my couch, a place from which I had not stirred in hours.

No computers, I was sure. Yet the door from which she had emerged was marked CAD, black letters on rippled glass. Puzzling.

We had to stop meeting like this. I smiled, she ever startled by my eyes before she knew I watched.

The words echoed in my mind: "It's hard to find us, it's not impossible."

Others had been there. So many others that they called us clients, and were neither surprised nor frightened by our appearance at the office.

Clients? Customers? She had assumed I was a designer. Why would an airplane company in a parallel time have designers in our time for clients?

I narrowed my eyes at the fire. Keep it simple, Richard. Simple logic.

Because it performs some service to designers.

What possible service . . . ? The fire burned lower. What service had Saunders-Vixen performed for me?

I caught my breath. The designs, of course! Each time I was stuck with a problem in design for the Cub—the door latch, the oil cap retainer—I woke in the morning with an answer already finished!

Saunders-Vixen, somehow, is in the business of . . . what? Psychic communication?

61

Intuition amplifiers? Breakthroughs? Saunders-
Vixen provides sudden breakthroughs for airplane designers who are stuck on some problem?
They have built an entire company in an alternate time in order to give me a free door
latch?

Somehow that did not strike me as wholly
rational, and finally I gave up. What did it matter? The fascination now was in going back, to
explore what the company might be, and perhaps to meet the mind behind that face that had
so charmed me, the woman in CAD.

Hard to find, not impossible. The fire settled gradually into coals. Times in my life, I am
struck by how important it is not to make things
too difficult for ourselves.

Richard, I thought, as one thinks to a six-
year-old, how did you find the place before?

Why, I lay down under the wing of the Cub
and imagined that I was drifting into another
time . . .

And how, I thought patiently, do you suppose you might find your way back?

By lying down under the wing . . .

Patiently: Do you need the Cub? Is the physical wing required?

By making myself very comfortable, I thought, by closing my eyes and imagining . . . There was no further prompting from my inner adult.

I settled into the couch. One slow, deep breath to relax my body. One slow, deep breath to relax my mind, clear the screen of all thought.

One slow, deep breath to remember where I had been . . . The fire disappeared.

"Hallo, are you still with us?" Derek Hawthorne reached to steady my shoulder. "You're flickering, a bit."

I shook my head. "Fine, thank you," I said. "I'm fine."

The woman looked at me softly, those dark

eyes. "It gets easier, the more you practice," she said.

Hawthorne watched her, watched me. "Miss Bristol, may I have the pleasure of introducing Mr. Richard Bach."

"Laura," she said, offering her hand.

Hawthorne nearly gasped at the informality.

"We've met," she added, a smile for his astonishment.

"We have," I said.

She was not tall, the top of her head to my shoulder, her face turned upward, the smile.

She didn't look nearly so businesslike as she had in the flash that we had met before.

"Your door latch," she said. "Is it working?"

"Yes! Working perfectly."

"You'll probably not want to do loops with the door open," she said. "The wind could bend the windowframe, at very high speed."

"But the latch won't fail, will it?"

She looked at me evenly. "The latch will not fail."

Hawthorne cleared his throat. "I was about to give our guest a tour . . ." As far as I could tell, he remained thunderstruck that Ms. Bristol had allowed me the shocking intimacy of her given name.

I wished the moment to last. "Why leather, for the oil cap retainer? Did you design it?"

"If design is the word," she said. "I suggested leather because it would be easier, it's cheaper than steel cable, it has no fatigue

65

limits, it can be replaced in the field, anywhere, it requires no special tools to install, there will be no sharp strands breaking, as it wears. It seemed the simplest solution to your problem, and likely the most practical.'' She paused. ''Of course . . .''

''Of course what, Ms. Bristol?'' I asked.

She frowned, puzzled. ''Of course you might tighten the oil cap, before you fly.''

''If it happened once,'' I told her, ''it will happen again. I shall keep my oil cap retainer as it is, thank you.''

''You're welcome.'' There the smile again, pleased that I liked her design. She leaned toward me, almost whispered. ''I think Mr. Hawthorne wants to show you the company.''

''I want to see it,'' I told her. ''You'll tell me about CAD, sometime?''

''It would be my pleasure.'' She nodded to my guide. ''Good day, Mr. Hawthorne.'' With that, she turned and left the two of us in the

hallway.

There was a long silence, the both of us watching her.

"Well, yes," said the young man at last, recovering his composure. "First, Mr. Bach, I suppose you'd like to see the hangar."

"Call me Richard," I said.

8

Stretched out, completely relaxed, on the couch in front of the fire, I knew that I could wake at any time. Yet I wanted to learn all I could about this strange place. Whether it was in my mind or reachable through my mind, whether it was objective or subjective didn't matter. Saunders-Vixen was real enough, un-predictable enough, its people submerged me deeply enough in new ideas and sweet mystery that the physics of the encounter didn't matter.

The main hangar, at the end of the long paneled walk, was filled with the quiet din of manufacture; the screech and clank of steel tube, the whir of bandsaws here, the whuffle and pop of fabric and rib-stitch needles there. Airplanes began as skeletons, gradually took shape as Derek Hawthorne walked me down the line. They were de Havilland *Tiger Moths*.

Briefly, I discovered that the Saunders-Vixen Aircraft Company, Ltd., is not in the business of supplying ideas to stumped airplane designers in a different time. That is one of its services, but the company exists to build airplanes to market in its own time.

"This is our A-line," Hawthorne said. "We build the *Kitten* training plane, as you can see, the SV-6F. These are fuselage jigs, of course, then if you look away down-line you see the wing sections joining the process at that big sign there, at E-station.

"Here at Duxford, we also build the *Arrow* mailplane, that's the SV-15, and the '21C *Empress*, our twin-engine passenger transport. They have their own assembly hangars."

"They're all biplanes?"

"Of course. When you want strong, when you want reliable, you want a biplane. At least that's my thought."

As we walked down the line, I could see the airplanes taking shape. Then it struck me.

"You call them *Kittens*?"

He nodded gravely. "The SV-6F. Yes. Wait till you pop in one, take it for a turn. It's a marvelous little machine."

"But they're *Tiger Moths*, aren't they? Built by de Havilland?"

He hadn't heard. "You'll notice we've moved the centre-section forward, to make it not quite such a bother for the instructor to slip in and out the cockpit. That gives us our rather lovely swept wing on top, to keep the centre of pressure where it belongs . . ."

73

"But these are *Tiger Moths,* aren't they, Derek? Not *Kittens.*"

"They're whatever Mr. de Havilland wants to name them, in your time. He's a client, of course, quite a bright fellow."

"Are you telling me that Geoffrey de Havilland? Copied? The design? Of your airplane? And called it his?"

Hawthorne frowned. "Nothing of the sort. A designer wrestles with a problem till he's beastly tired. He drowses. He daydreams. He sleeps. And all at once, there's his answer! He jots it down on an envelope, some scrap of vellum that's handy, and he's fixed his problem! Where do you suppose the answers come from?"

My voice caught on the word. "Here?"

"The best designers are the ones who know when to stop knitting their brows and relax, who know how to let a new drawing use their hands to put itself on paper."

"And the designs come from here."

"From the CAD, yes."

"From . . . ?"

"The Crosstime Assistance Division, Saunders-Vixen Aircraft Company, Limited. We're only too glad to help." He touched my shoulder, pointed to wing panels wheeling by on a dolly, pushed by an assembler in white coveralls, the company logo embroidered in black.

"Look here. We call them 'slats.' At low speed, the slats pop open, the airstream slips up behind them, over the top of the wing, and instead of stalling the wingtips, you've got more lift. A bit of smart, don't you think?"

75

I was stuck on a different thought. "Are the airplanes your designs, or his?"

He turned to me, earnest to explain. "The design exists, Richard, the possibility of just this combination of elements in just these relationships, the design for this machine existed at the very instant that spacetime began. Whoever first draws the plans gets to call it whatever they want to call it. Every world has its own laws and ideas about who owns what, they're mostly different."

He frowned, concentrating. "We call the design *Kitten,* and in our world it's a Saunders-Vixen SV-6F, duly patented and protected by law. Geoffrey de Havilland, in his time, that is, in what you call your past, calls it *Tiger Moth,* patented in the name of de Havilland Aircraft Company. Genevieve de la Roche, in her time, calls it *Papillon,* registered under the marque of Avions la Roche. You understand, don't you? There's no end to it."

Hawthorne was nearly out of words. He was

worried, I thought, that somehow I still didn't follow.

"You see, the design doesn't care," he said. "The design is the invisible structure for a grand kite, always has been, always will be, whether or not anyone discovers it. And it flies like a fox!" He smiled. "As we like to say around here."

"You're very good, Derek," I said. "Before too long I might actually understand what you're talking about."

He looked at me for a second, concerned blue eyes. A quick smile. "Me too."

Near the end of the line the pieces came together for assembly in rainbows of customer colors. Company markings on some, pilots' and owners' names on others, a series of school planes with sequential letters, tall bold capitals *J, K, L* on the rudders.

Outside, the sound of engines starting, running up, falling back to idle.

What a feeling that must be, I thought, to

77

arrive at the factory one day to take delivery of one's own wood-and-cloth biplane, brand-new!

"The engines, I suppose, are not Rolls-Royce Gipsy Majors."

"What do you think?"

"No," I said.

"We use the Trevayne Mark 2 *Circe*."

"Of course. I'd call it a Gipsy Major."

"You would," he said, solemnly.

We chatted on about the airplanes, stopping now and then as he pointed out clever parts of the machines he thought I might not have noticed.

He didn't seem to know that I was as much fascinated by his time as by his aircraft.

"This is not 1923, is it?"

He cocked his head, puzzled. "Of course it's 1923. To us. It's our 1923."

"The Tiger Moth wasn't invented until 1930-something. Early 1930-something."

"Do use *discovered*, would you? *Invented*, well, it seems so . . . proprietary, somehow. The design has always been there."

"The Tiger Moth wasn't discovered until early 1930-something, Derek. What's it doing in 1923? Your 1923 is different from mine, I'll bet you're going to say."

"Quite," he said.

"You had a war, I believe," he said. "You call it the Great War? Well, we didn't. Quite a number of us saw it coming and decided not to be part of it. The waste."

He didn't sound sad, saying that, and I realized that he had nothing to feel sad about. He didn't know what destruction looked like.

"Declining the war, we split away into an alternate time, where we could concentrate on doing what we enjoy. In our case, of course, Saunders-Vixen's, that was discovering aeroplane designs. So some of our 'planes came a bit earlier than yours, as we didn't have to muck about with warplanes along the way, have our designers killed at the Front, all that rubbish.''

''. . . split away into an alternate time?''

''Of course. Happens every minute, people decide to change their future. You decided not to have a nuclear war, in what I guess was your 1963. You came close, but decided not to. Quite a few others made a different decision, that a war would meet their needs. Different times: diverging, converging, parallel. Ours are parallel.''

''Which is why I can visit.''

''No. You can visit because you love the same things we do. You like boffing about in a first-class two-winger. We like building them.''

''Simple as that.''

''Almost,'' he said. ''And we're safe.''

''You're safe.''

''Indeed,'' he said. He stopped at the wing of a daisy-yellow Kitten, at the very end of the production line, brushed a speck of invisible dust from the British roundel painted on the fuselage. "You're attracted here because we're enough like your own past to be known. There's no question how it will work out, here. This world's not soon to go up in flames. You can count on Saunders-Vixen's time to have big grass aerodromes dotting the countryside, air circuses flying hither and fro, hopping passengers a few shillings the ride, engines and air-frames simple enough, straightforward enough a pilot can work on them with a spanner or two, patch a hole with fabric and dope, leave your degree in electronics and high-energy physics at home."

"I can't get killed here, flying?"

"It's possible, I suppose." He spoke as if he hadn't considered it before. "There is the odd crash, now and then. Nobody much seems to get hurt, though." He brightened. "We like to think it's because we build quite a fine machine."

He led the way through a door in the hangar wall, and in a moment we were blinking in sunlight. It was a sight that both burned into my memory and evoked it at the same time, as though I had been here before.

At the white concrete parking ramp the grass took over, green as an inland sea, lapping at the hardsurface. It spread in a vast rural square about us, and in the distance the green lifted in slow gentle swells, quilted by farm-lands, blossomed in oaks.

It was a flyer's paradise. Whichever direc-tion the wind, there was soft grass underwheel for landing. This was history before the inven-tion of narrow crosswind runways, a delight for the eye and heart.

There must have been twenty Kittens on the hard surface, most of them older working ma-chines in for maintenance, some just rolled from the production line, waiting a pilot for their first flight test. One was lettered SAUNDERS-VIXEN SCHOOL OF FLYING down the fuselage, an instructor and student settling into the two cockpits, one passing a folded aerial chart to the other. At the far end of the line, dwarfing the trainers, stood a graceful cabin bi-plane that must have been the *Empress.*

Closest to us, though, was one of the latest aircraft from the Kitten production line, cowling open, an engineer done with adjusting the carburetor, moving his toolbox clear.

I stood with Hawthorne and waited for the engine start, enjoying the morning and the moment.

"A few turns?" the pilot said, from the cockpit.

It was a lovely airplane, lace-white with gold chevrons arrowing forward along the top surfaces. On the aft fuselage the registration letters: G-EMLF.

"Eight blades through," said the engineer, grasping the black wooden propeller by one blade. "Switch off?"

"Switch off," said the pilot.

He pulled the propeller around by hand, clockwise.

"Our engines turn the wrong way to yours," said Hawthorne just above a whisper, explaining what might have looked strange to his visitor. In a moment he corrected. "I don't mean ours Saunders-Vixen, of course, I mean ours British."

I nodded, and liked the man for what he said. He cared to make things as right as he knew how.

"Any time," said the ground engineer.

"Contact!" We heard the brassy clack of the magneto switch under the pilot's glove.

The engineer swung the propeller briskly through a single rotation, there came a lazy burst of oil-smoke from one cylinder, another, a silent revolution or two, then three cylinders were firing, then finally all four lit off, blue-gray smoke blown back, fragmenting, in the spiral wind.

I watched the pilot, leather-helmeted, nod to the engineer, thumbs-up thanks for a good start, as the quick thunder settled to an easy slow idle, missing a beat now and then, for the cold engine.

That moment I wished time could turn to crystal, wished it to stop in the cool morning, the gentle sound of the machine, the promise of liftoff, of flight over this lovely countryside, of returning again out of the air onto the land, a whisper on the grass.

Obediently, time did just that. Not quite stop, but turned slow motion as I savored the air, the color, the little plane. I watched the broad propeller's disk, glittering white sunflash, heard the sound of polished wood against cool air, shuffled with the engine's slow chaffs.

Here it is, I thought, I am looking this moment at the magnet of flight. One pole is black-iron engines and sheet cloth wings, easy to touch. The other is life and freedom in the sky, the breath of spirit on our hands. That

moment I saw them both, felt their enchant-
ments tug at my body. *Come,* they whispered,
you can fly!

I wanted to stay in the frame of that painting
forever.

So slowly, the engineer walked back to stand
by the cockpit, and two heads bent over the in-
strument panel. Then gradually the sound in-
creased, throttle forward, the little Kitten
straining against its wheel chocks, the air-hush
of the propeller lost in the serious power of an
engine at three-quarter speed.

It held that power for a long moment, sharp
wind-bursts beating the engineer's white coveralls, the black SAUNDERS-VIXEN between his
shoulders rippled to a blur.

At last the engineer nodded, and slowly the
power fell back again to idle, the four cylinders
warm and wide awake, no missed beats.

After a minute the engine suddenly
switched off, the propeller turning alone on its
own for long seconds, the muffled clank of

86

oiled connecting rods inside the engine slowing, finally, to stop.

The pilot swept her helmet off, the better to hear the conversation. Dark hair cascaded about her shoulders as she asked, concerned, for the engineer's verdict.

I blinked, so unexpected the sight. "This isn't heaven, is it, Hawthorne?"

"Not far from it," he said, "if you like aeroplanes."

We walked toward the lace-and-gold trainer.

"How many people from my time . . . from other times, visit here?"

He looked upward for a moment, guessing. "Quite a few, actually. The ones who like to imagine, who enjoy the play, they make it across rather well. Of course it gets easier, as you know, every time."

"Flyers, all of them?"

"Most. You'd expect that, of course. Duxford's a flyer's town, what with Saunders-

Vixen and an aerodrome on the doorstep. If one loved the sea, I fancy they'd show up round Portsmouth, Copenhagen, Marseilles.'' He shrugged. ''It's not as if one needs a passport. Anybody can come, who loves it here. A few decide to stay . . .'' He let the sentence die.

''When it gets too hard at home?''

''I shouldn't say so. After a time, they prefer it here. Possibly it's the climate.''

I looked to him sharply, saw his smile.

''Do you ever visit our time, Derek?''

He laughed. ''Never. I'm too much the pussy-cat, I should say, for your rough-and-tumble.''

Instead of interrupting the conversation at the warm Kitten, he turned back to the hangar, past the production line, no one giving us a glance. ''We've only just begun your tour,'' he said. ''The company has divisions you can't imagine. I'm still finding out, myself.''

''Still finding out?''

"We make aeroplanes first of all, but we're quite a bit the service company, as well."

There was a long silence, waiting for him to continue.

". . . service company, as well . . ." I prodded.

"We solve problems."

"Airplane design problems."

"Yes, but not just. Other problems."

After a moment, I said, "And I'm going to have to drag it out of you."

"Probably so."

He opened the door for me, back into the long paneled hallway that led to the reception room, and the noise of the factory faded. The aircraft in the paintings along the way were mostly familiar to me. All were Saunders-Vixen designs.

"Plenty of time for discovery," he said at last. "Unless you plan never to return. In which case there's no point finding out, is there?"

Presently he slowed at the door marked

CAD. "One moment," he said. "I shall find your tour guide, Phase Two."

While I waited, I examined the paintings. Here, a scene of a Piper Cub, a mirror of my own, the same bright yellow, and a caption: *Saunders-Vixen K-1 Chickadee.*

No other difference I could tell, scrutinizing the art, save that I knew that was no Continental engine painted there, like the one under the cowling of my Cub. If Hawthorne told me the Chickadee was powered by a Greeves *Bumble-Dart,* I wouldn't have blinked.

In time he appeared. "Miss Bristol seems not to be about," he said. "I'm sorry."

He led the way to the reception office.

"Like it or not, my visit's over?"

"For an early visit, you've lasted quite a while," he said, cheerfully enough. "So much new, you'll tire, you'll be fading soon. Nothing to be concerned about. Every time you can stay longer, if you wish."

I walked through the door he opened for me, back into the office.

On the counter at the reception desk was a small wicker basket of mints.

"Is there a fellow here named Gaines?" I asked.

"Why, yes, of course," said Hawthorne, startled. "Do you know Ian?"

I shrugged out of my jacket, handed it back to my host. "He has a pet project?"

"As a matter of fact, he does. It's a scheme, quite ingenious, really, quite simple. A colored light at the side of the runway, angled to show when one is dropping a bit low on the glide-path. He demonstrated it to the company brass just the other day. Everyone came away rather pleased with Mr. Gaines. He was happy as a cork."

I reached for a mint, on the reception counter, but it wasn't candy. It was a kind of pocket piece, the Saunders-Vixen company logo. A brass oval, with a propeller horizontal through the center. A handsome thing, I thought, to remind me of the place, make it easier to return.

"May I?"

The woman at the desk nodded. "Of course. But if you're from the other side, sir, it won't likely make it across. Nothing quite does. Just mind-stuff." She smiled. "So they tell me. What do I know?"

"You've never been across?"

She shook her head. "Duxford born and raised." Then, confidentially: "And learning to fly!"

"Would you care for me to join you out the door?" said Hawthorne. "Some do, some don't. Some want to see how far they can go up the path before they fade out. Odd, the tricks the mind can play."

"I'll try it alone," I said. "You'll be here next time, when I come back? Or will everyone be different?"

"Rest your mind. It'll be us. Of course, you've hardly seen the place. Tip of the iceberg, do you say? We're quite a large organisation, actually."

"Next time," I said. "Till then." I clenched the brass logo tightly in my fist. If it had to be lost, it wouldn't be for letting it go.

I turned and walked out the door I had entered less than an hour before, a curious warmth through me. I liked this place. I liked it a lot.

How far can I go? Out the covered walkway, down the steps, footsteps crunching on the gravel of the car-park. I turned and looked at the building once more, to fix it in my mind. The giant hangar, the offices in a tier, away from the aerodrome.

I had seen so little, I thought. A reception room, a hall, a hangar, a parking ramp. A glimpse of countryside. Why had she not been there, Laura Bristol, after offering to show me about?

93

How many people work for the company, and what do they do? A service organization, Hawthorne had said. What kind of service? Airplane design, yes. What else?

I made it back to the hill overlooking the aerodrome. The lace-and-gold Kitten had its cowling fastened down, the engine running again, a whisper across the distance, and now it moved toward the grass, taxiing for its first flight.

The scene didn't fade. I took a long look about. Next time, I thought, I will fly.

A deep breath, to relax my body. Another, relax my mind. Another, to . . .

"Richard!" A woman's voice, across the distance. "Richard, wait!"

I looked back down the path. Laura Bristol stood by the car-park, and when I turned, she waved. "Only a minute?" she called.

We met by the hedge along the path to the hangar. "I'm sorry I wasn't there, a bit ago,"

she said. "There was a meeting. I should so like
to have shown you about."

"Thank you," I said. "I should like to have
been shown. Next time?"

"I need your advice," she said. "Would you
mind, a moment?"

"As many moments as Whatever It Is lets me
stay," I said. A delight, I thought, to be invited
to watch those dark eyes for longer than a
glance.

"I'll be quick," she said. "The company has
offered me a position in partial-pressure disk
design. It's all quite exciting, but I wonder if
you . . . you're closer to that time. I wonder if
you think it might be a good idea."

"Partial-pressure disks? I'm afraid that
doesn't ring too many bells, for me."

She wasn't dismayed at my ignorance, hur-
ried to explain. "It's a system of aero-travel.
One controls the pressure on the surface of a
disk, and the atmosphere pushes the disk to-

ward the area of low pressure. One can move at very high speed, there is no factor of a sound-limit speed as the machine is not in fact moving through the air but through a partial vacuum in its midst . . ."

She saw my eyes and stopped. "It's beside the point," she said. "The point is that the work I've been offered is in a division of the company that's several centuries in the future. It remains parallel to your time, though, and I wondered if you might tell me if you like it, the time where you live? They've shown me a glimpse of that world, it's all quite exciting, but there's rather a lot of high technology about and I must say I'm not quite used to that."

I should have been able to tell her at least a strength and weakness or two of life in higher tech than Duxford's, but before courtesy engaged reason, I spoke.

"Don't go," I said.

Her eyes widened, her head tilted a question, her lips parted in surprise. "I wasn't asking for a decision, Richard. I was hoping you might . . ."

"How foolish of me," I said. "I'm sorry." I looked for an explanation, spoke it on sight. "Laura, I'm a refugee from technology. That's why I'm here. In the world I come from, my little Cub is nearly seventy years old, it's an antique. Everything else . . ."

She nodded. Did I need to say more?

"It's a big opportunity," she said.

"For what?" I said. "A big opportunity . . . ?"

"To learn. Grow. Change."

"You fly a Kitten, don't you?"

She nodded, perplexed. "The Company's quite keen on helping us fly. I did my A licence a year ago."

"So off you go into the twenty-third century, you design systems for disks that move at hyperspeed. Where's the wind?"

She studied my face.

"You'll miss it," I said. "The sound of four

97

cylinders and a wooden propeller, the sound of the wind in the flying-wires. And you'll miss the people here, the ones who know that music, the ones who build it.''

''And if I stay, you're going to ask, if I don't go to that century, will I miss the technology?'' The dark eyes did not leave mine.

''I would ask that.''

Softly a breeze touched us, brushed the grass, smoothing it, gentling it, settling it down to rest. Settled her, as well.

''One longs for what the heart's denied,'' she said.

''You didn't need advice at all, did you, Laura?''

''Oh, you're so wrong,'' she said quickly. Then she paused, thoughtful. ''You've been a great help. I shan't forget.'' To my astonishment, she stepped close and kissed my cheek.

I didn't stumble, but it felt that way, as though I slipped and fell from the branch of

some enchanted tree. Unhurt from the impact,
I opened my eyes.

The coals in the fireplace were gray feather-
fluffs under the grate. The old clock ticked.
Not an hour had passed.

Rain began outside, with the night. My fist,
tightly clenched around the brass of the company logo, was empty. Opposite to my heart,
strangely full.

Laura Bristol would make the decision that
she chose to make, I thought, and whatever it
was, it would be the right choice for her.

I moved to the fireplace, set one piece of
wood over the coals.

In forty years flying I've met thousands of
airplane pilots, I thought, thousands more who
love the sky. How many had found this place
before me? How many here and now, who slip
off to Saunders-Vixen for the fun of it, slide
gently across to fly on air vastly simpler than
ours, in different sunlight, to work on flying-

machines that in our time don't exist, to meet friends and loves they've missed here? Unless they told me, how would I know where they'd been?

Overlapping this room, alongside this minute, floats the village of Duxford, war-free. No matter what happens in my twenty-first century, just three breaths away stand the hangars of the Saunders-Vixen Aircraft Company, Ltd., safe in its year 1923, a past waiting to be my future the moment I imagine the journey. There live Derek Hawthorne and Laura Bristol

and scores of others unmet, engineers and businessfolk, designers and flyers, from whom I yet have much to learn.

Hawthorne was right. It is rough-and-tumble, our world, it's no place for pussycats.

But somehow, I thought, I'm glad I found his land, I'm glad I have a choice.

—END—